A MINDSET MAP

Shift Your Perspective
and Transform Your Life

Belinda Egan

ISBN: 979-8-218-08701-2

Praise for

A Mindset Map Shift Your Perspective, Transform Your Life

"*Mindset Map* is exactly what you need to take a look at yourself. In this book, Belinda shares her personal journey and asks powerful questions to help you discover where your mindset might need an adjustment. Her straightforward, concise, and helpful ideas will guide you as you open yourself up to the possibility of change. This book will challenge you to do the work and create a mindset that works for you."

— **Tammy Helfrich,** Author of *Unapologetic* &
Host of the Intentional Life Podcast

"Belinda Egan hits home with her insights in *A Mindset Map.* Each chapter builds on the previous and guides the reader through a different life perspective lesson. The journey comes from a place of experience, love, and the desire to help others. Belinda shares personal experiences in a way that resonates and helps focus the lesson. These deep insights are followed by questions to allow the reader to look inside themselves, which is crucial to the mindset journey. Her desire to help and bring value to others and her knowledge and experience in Leadership shine through in *A Mindset Map.* I highly recommend diving in!"

— **Kitty Stolle,** Regional Special Investigative
Unit Manager, GEICO (Retired)

"Mindset is powerful and can impact many areas of your life—for better or worse. In *Mindset Map*, Belinda Egan challenges your mindset and leads you on a path to true transformation. Whether you're looking to show up differently personally or professionally, Belinda will help you shift your perspective and transform your life. At the end of each chapter, she challenges you to dive in and 'Do the Work'—the work that will lead you to become your authentic self. As Belinda says, 'Act as if you're already living in your future. Be the person you want to be in your new life.' You can start making simple shifts TODAY! I highly recommend this book for anyone feeling stuck and ready to take their life or business to the next level."

— **Hailey Krajewski**

Dedication and Gratitude

For my daughter, Savannah Rae Egan: You are my greatest joy and most significant challenge wrapped up in one big bundle of love. I'm so thankful that God chose me to be your mom. You've taught me how to love unconditionally and helped me grow into the person I am today. Because of you, I wanted to do better. I want you to know that you can accomplish anything you set your mind to. You have the power within you to do big things. The world needs that special something that only you have. Always dream big, baby girl.

For John: You've always been my biggest supporter—always believing in me and pushing me to believe in myself. Without you, none of this would be possible. Your love, support, patience, and encouragement have given me the strength to go after my dreams.

For Judy and Tracy: Thank you for always showing up. I know many people, but I have only a few great friends. From listening to "Total Eclipse of the Heart" while practicing our bubble letters to getting in trouble for those five AM "birthday" parties to being able to pick up where we left off no matter how much time passed, I know that I'll never be alone because there are two fantastic women that will pull out that ponytail holder to have my back without hesitation. Thank you for showing up. Thank you for being my friends.

You've made the dash between my birth and death more meaningful, and I'm forever grateful.

For My Parents: I now understand. Thank you for choosing life. Thank you for giving up your dreams to ensure ours had a chance. I know now that every family has its challenges. That parenting is hard. That life throws us curveballs, and how we pivot matters. I know now that we each have a lens that tints, shades, and at times warps how we see things. I now understand that we all do the best we can.

For my big brother, Rey: Thank you for always being the voice of reason. You've always been the go-to sibling in the family. Thank you for taking on that tremendous responsibility and, most of all, for not giving up on me.

Contents

Introduction
Shift Your Perspective, Transform Your Life

"Let the wisdom of lessons learned
be your hope for the future."
Belinda Egan

This book was initially meant to be "50 Life Lessons from 50 Years of Living," but during the writing and editing process, I realized that most of the lessons I had learned throughout my life had a similar thread running through them: To really understand the lesson, I had to shift my mindset and understanding.

In all areas of my life, the single most significant positive shift has always taken place when I change my mind— look at something from a different perspective—and try it another way.

It seems so simple in theory, but it takes a lifetime of work in practice.

So, for each chapter of this book, I've included a "Do the Work" section where you can put your new mindset shift into practice.

Here's how you'll know when the hard work is paying off:
If you feel uncomfortable, your mindset is shifting. If it feels
scary and you're unsure if you can do it, you're headed in the
right direction. Keep pushing.

Here's to changing your mind, a little bit, every day.

Love,

Belinda

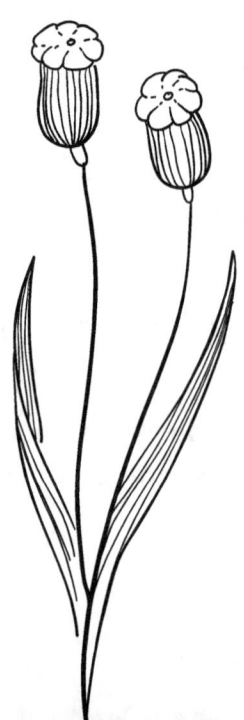

Anger Doesn't Solve Problems— It Creates Them

You're in a heated argument with someone you care about. You're talking fast, shooting from the hip. You feel your back is against the wall—like you must prove you're right.

At this point, you've already lost the fight. You're entirely in your feelings now, not listening to the other person. There's no room for understanding.

Suddenly, you feel heat rush to your face as you spit out words that you know will hurt.

You see the betrayal immediately cross the eyes of the person you care about. Their body tenses up. They begin to slump and pull away from you.

It might have felt good to say it in the moment, but now it feels awful. You've just said something you can't take back. You've just slung mud. It's not a great look for you.

No problems have been solved… and a new one has been created.

There are two parts to overcoming anger to solve a problem with someone else: understanding *what* has made you angry and *why* it's made you angry.

When you feel your emotions rushing ahead of your thoughts, take a breath. Pause. Don't speak again until you've taken a nice deep breath.

Determine which part, if any, of this situation you can control. If you have zero control, it's time to put down the mud and walk away.

Conversations, heated debates, and even arguments serve a purpose: to better understand yourself and the other person. And nothing gets in the way of a shared understanding faster than anger and resentment.

Find the hidden gem of understanding by being patient, listening more than you speak, and taking as many breaths as needed. This takes practice; but in time, you can transform your anger into a better understanding of yourself and the people around you.

Do the Work
Understand Your Anger

What is your first reaction when you get angry? Do you attack or withdraw? Do you feel like you lose control, or do you feel like you can take a step back from it without reacting to it right away?

If you can take a step back from the anger, take a closer look at what caused this sudden rush of emotion. Is there another feeling there? Remember to breathe while you process this. Take your time. Get quiet and listen to your inner voice.

What feeling or memory comes to mind when you think about angry reactions in your life? Write this feeling or memory down. Think about how this feeling or memory is connected to your current anger. A strong emotional response to a situation from the past usually indicates there's still some healing to do around this situation.

Whenever possible, try to lengthen the time between your instantaneous feeling of anger and your reaction to it. This will take time and practice. Celebrate each time you're able to feel and not react, even if it's only for a few seconds at a time!

Journal Notes

Chapter Two

Here's Where Your Actions and Inactions Have Brought You

In 2005, I ran my first marathon.

Signing up was easy. I was filled with exuberance, optimism, and premature pride about my decision. "Belinda Egan, Marathon Runner" had a nice ring to it.

But convincing myself to get out there and train every day was another thing entirely—one which was much harder to do over and over.

Did you know there's a specific label for people who don't finish marathons? The ones who sign up but never train, train but not hard enough, or run but not long enough to finish the race?

Yeah… once I found that out, it lit a fire in me. I didn't want to be *that* person labeled DNF (Did Not Finish).

So, I dragged myself out of bed. I hit the pavement. I trained myself to the point of exhaustion. When marathon day came, I was ready. And I pushed through the whole marathon to the finish line. What a fantastic feeling that was!

That feeling was the culmination of a thousand actions—
good choices—that helped me reach the end of the marathon.

What's your marathon story?

Well... you're living it right now.

Where you are today is a direct reflection of your choices.

Anytime you start to feel like you have no control over your
journey, just take a second to think about the decisions
you've made (both good and bad) and where they've led you.

And then take a moment to think about the decisions you
haven't made and how *they've* affected your trajectory.

You have total control over your decisions; and whether or
not you make them, your life changes.

Drinking and driving. Saving for retirement. Taking that
fabulous job opportunity out of state. Saying hi to that
attractive stranger. Do you, or don't you?

Whether you do or don't, something changes. Action or
inaction—a reaction always occurs.

And the reaction is your life.

So, what will you do next?

Do the Work
Adding Up Your Actions and Inactions

Think about the last time you decided to put effort into something, even if it was as small as cleaning up a room in your house. What was the action, and what was the thinking process that led you to do it? Was it a list of pros and cons? Or maybe you just "played the tape forward" to think about the consequences of not doing the thing? Write down your action and your list of reasons for doing it.

Now, think about a time you decided *not* to do something. Write down your inaction and the reasons you chose not to do it.

Think about both this action and inaction. Is there a common theme between why you did and didn't do these things? Maybe you're trying to be healthier, be easier on yourself in general, or be more productive in a certain way. If you're intentional about both your actions and inactions, you'll find that both are working toward a goal, mission, or purpose in your life. Write down your observations about this.

Journal Notes

_____

_____

_____

_____

_____

_____

_____

_____

_____

_____

_____

_____

_____

_____

_____

_____

_____

_____

Chapter Three
Save Your "Cares" for What Matters

There's a gal I know whose husband passed away from ALS. They had lived with this insidious disease for over two years before it took him.

Shortly after he died, she met someone and started dating him. They soon became a couple and made it public.

People in her social circle judged her for having moved on too quickly.

The question that came to mind was, "Why does it matter?"

I only have a certain amount of emotional bandwidth in a given day, and I try to make an active effort to save it for things that really matter: the health of my family, my personal fulfillment, working hard to be a better person, and enjoying life's simple pleasures.

If someone in my life has made a choice that doesn't affect me, hurt me, or cause any upheaval to my life, why should I spend my precious bandwidth caring about that decision? I literally cannot afford to; it would be stealing emotional bandwidth from other much more important aspects of my life.

If you find yourself feeling any emotional reaction to a choice someone else makes, practice asking yourself these things:

- Does this person's choice cause me any problems personally?

- Will it affect my personal health or the health of my family?

- Will I experience any fallout from their decision?

If the answer to any of these is "no," you can choose to let go of this issue and move on. In fact, it's vital that you do so! Remember that *spending* care on something that doesn't affect you personally is *stealing* care from more important things.

It may take practice if you're in the habit of concerning yourself with others' choices, but it will be worth it. You will feel freer and lighter as you choose to let people live their lives in peace... and reserve your own "cares" for the important stuff.

Life is hard enough without worrying about what everybody else is doing. So simply don't! It's not worth it—literally.

Do the Work
Saving Your Cares for the Big Stuff

Take a moment to remember some of the things you've spent a lot of time thinking and caring about this week. On balance, how many of these things were all about your own life? And how many were about other people's lives?

If you've found yourself *spending a care* on someone else's decisions or actions, notice how you're taking away from the quality of *care* that you can then direct to your own life. Ask yourself: Is it worth it?

Continue to check your "care balance" throughout the day by asking yourself: Is this affecting the quality of my life or someone else's? If it's affecting the quality of someone else's life, ask yourself: Can I afford to spend care to help?

Journal Notes

Chapter Four
"No" is a Complete Sentence

Saying "no" without an apology or an explanation shouldn't be so hard. But for most of us, it often is.

I've struggled to say "no" for lots of reasons: the fear of disappointing someone, the fear of missing out on an opportunity, the worry that I'll feel guilty, or sometimes simply just feeling like I *owe* someone a "yes" instead of a "no."

A friend once told me a little story that changed my feelings about "no."

"When I was a little girl," she said, "a friend of mine called and asked me if I could go over and play. I asked my mom, and she said 'no.' So, I told my friend that I wasn't able to. My friend asked me why. I turned to my mother and said, 'My friend wants to know why I've said *no*.' My mom said, 'You don't have to give her a reason or make up an excuse. Just say no.'"

These days, when I need or want to say "no," I do it without hesitation, without explaining, and certainly without an exaggerated made-up excuse.

If you feel compelled to apologize for saying "no," you can replace it with a "thank you": "I can't make it, but thank you for thinking of me!"

"No" can be a complete sentence. Practice feeling confident about it!

Do the Work
Your History of "Yes" When It Should Have Been "No"

Why do you struggle to say "no," even when you really want to?

Do you feel like you fairly judge how critical a situation is before saying "yes" to it?

What would it take for you to prioritize saying "no" to things that just don't matter to your life?

Journal Notes

_____

_____

_____

_____

_____

_____

_____

_____

_____

_____

_____

_____

_____

_____

_____

_____

_____

_____

Chapter Five
Wholeheartedness Begins with a Broken Heart

2016 was a year of exponential growth for me. It was the year I found my center of gravity as a person.

The previous three years had brought me a lot of turmoil and heartache. I had gotten to a point in my life where I was simply struggling to survive. I was drinking too much. I was angry all the time. I was incredibly depressed.

All the drinking and focusing on negative emotions came to a head one day when I found that I couldn't get out of bed. All I wanted to do was sleep and not face the world around me.

Depression was new to me. I'd never been one to suffer from any melancholy, so the sheer force of will I had to exercise to get anything done was a shocker to me.

I could function enough to get through the days, but I couldn't wait to crawl back into bed at the end of the day and stop thinking... stop trying.

Life had broken my heart.

Thankfully, one day, just as suddenly as this foul depression had come upon me, I realized it was time to snap out of it.

I realized that I had wasted precious time "surviving" instead of living.

It was time to pull myself up and get on with the business of living—and figure out how to do it well.

I knew I needed a clear mind to work through the issues plaguing my mind and heart. So, the first thing I did was decide to stop drinking.

While alcohol itself isn't a long-term issue for me (and I happily enjoy a cold margarita now and then), I abstained from alcohol for about a year; and it was so worth it. The clarity I found was nothing short of astounding. It was the right move for that period in my life.

I also limited my contact with people in general. I needed time to just sit with all that was going on in my mind and heart. I took daily walks by myself to learn to be present and left my phone at home; it was just me, blue skies, and sunshine. I walked every day for a year.

During these walks, my brain began to sort out a lot of stuff. I started to see meaning in who I was and where I'd come from. Best of all, I could more clearly see where I was going.

It was a highly productive twelve months. I read books, wrote, went to therapy, and dealt with my emotional baggage.

In *The Gifts of Imperfection*, Brené Brown says, "Wholehearted living is about engaging in our lives from a place of worthiness. It means cultivating the courage, compassion, and connection to wake up in the morning and think, 'No matter what gets done and how much is left undone, I am enough.'"

The first thing I learned over my year of "reset" was to show up and accept whoever I was that day. This takes work. Sometimes, it's hard to look in the mirror and say, "I'm not feeling so hot about myself today, but that's okay."

The second thing I learned is that my life situation directly reflects my feelings of self-worth. So, if I wanted to reset correctly, I had to start fostering a real sense of self-worth.

It took time. It took patience. Some days, it really hurt. But over time, I began to feel like I was living wholeheartedly. Honestly. Vulnerably.

Today, I show up in my life as imperfect, and I'm not afraid to show my true self to the world. I didn't have a *Leave It to Beaver* upbringing, and I don't pretend I did. My family is dysfunctional, as is every other family I know. These days, I strive to be as authentic as possible and embrace my imperfect life. It took work, but I can confidently say I'm proud of who I am, where I've come from, and where I'm headed.

If you don't feel good about yourself right now, that's okay. Embrace it. Accept it. This is the beginning of change.

Wholeheartedness always begins with a broken heart.

Do the Work
Practicing Wholeheartedness

Do you feel shame about things in your past, experiences, or character flaws? Be very honest with yourself. Find the shame and shine a light on it. Sit with it. Don't be afraid; the fear of your shame is worse than actually sitting with it.

What kind of feeling comes up when you think about releasing that shame and accepting the thing that gives you shame?

Envision your version of a Wholehearted You living a Wholehearted Life. What kinds of things does this version of you take joy in? What steps can you take to head in the direction of Wholeheartedness today? What is the first thing you can do to start your journey?

Journal Notes

Chapter Six

Forgiveness of Others is a Gift to Yourself

You've most likely been in plenty of situations where you had the choice to forgive someone for hurting you, either directly or indirectly.

Often, the thoughts that go through our minds sound like, "If I forgive this person, will they turn around and hurt me again?" or, "Should I forgive and forget, or just forgive and be more careful about trusting this person next time?"

Both these questions come at the idea of forgiveness by trying to gauge how your forgiveness will affect the *other* person. But how many times have you thought about how extending forgiveness to someone else benefits or hurts *you*?

When you choose not to forgive someone, you may feel like you're teaching them a lesson or returning hurt for hurt, but the truth is that the damage you do to yourself by not forgiving is tenfold.

Here's why: Forgiveness means you choose not to hold onto the anger, hurt, and bitterness that comes from not offering forgiveness. Whether or not you want to, if you don't forgive, you end up ruminating on the event and your sense of betrayal. It doesn't feel good. It poisons your "inner well of peace."

But choosing to forgive is a gift for the person who caused the hurt and for you: the gift of compassion, understanding, growth, perspective, and freedom from rumination and doubt and mistrust.

And the most surprisingly enjoyable part of offering forgiveness is this one: When you forgive, you find that you can gently and graciously accept forgiveness when it's inevitably extended to you.

Do the Work
The Lessons of Forgiveness

Imagine facing the choice to forgive someone close to you for something that shattered your trust in them. Maybe you've experienced this already! Write down the thoughts, feelings, doubts, and questions that came up about extending forgiveness. Don't hold back or censor yourself. Write everything that comes to mind.

Have you noticed a pattern of questions that come up repeatedly when you choose to forgive people in your life?

Have you refused to forgive someone in your life? How did that make you feel?

Do you see any ways you can work on yourself to be freer in forgiving yourself and others?

What steps can you take today to work on that healing?

Journal Notes

_____

_____

_____

_____

_____

_____

_____

_____

_____

_____

_____

_____

_____

_____

_____

_____

_____

_____

_____

_____

_____

Chapter Seven
Would You Rather Have a Clean Room or an Empty One?

There was a time during my daughter's high school years when she and I were clashing about everything under the sun.

It was a really challenging period in our lives, as my husband and her father had recently been diagnosed with ALS (Amyotrophic Lateral Sclerosis). We were all trying to navigate this devastating news in our own way and hadn't quite found our bearings.

Having had a tumultuous relationship with my own mother, it wasn't something I wanted for my daughter and myself. And yet, despite my best intentions, I felt disconnected from her during this time; it was new to me, as we'd always had a very close relationship.

I decided that it was time for all of us to go to family counseling.

During one of our sessions, I brought up that I felt our daughter didn't respect that I liked to keep a clean and organized home, as her room was always a disaster. I would go out of my way to clean her room, fold her clothes, and put them away; but within less than twenty-four hours, it was right back to the state of disaster. It was incredibly frustrating for me. She and I had recently gotten into such a lousy argument about this one night that she left to stay at a friend's house for a few days.

When I told the therapist this, she asked me, "Would you rather have a clean room or an empty room?"

Ouch. I'd never thought of it that way.

But I instantly knew the answer: I'd take a disorganized, dirty, chaotic room over an empty room any day.

This was a turning point for my daughter and me. I think she needed to hear these wise words as much as I did.

We agreed, going forward, that our daughter would do her part in helping keep our home clean and organized; and I reveled in the gratitude that I had an occupied room instead of an empty one.

I've applied this lesson to so many aspects of my life: when my husband doesn't clean the kitchen up as well as I'd like; when one of my friends drives me crazy; when anyone close to me does something that irritates the living crap out of me. I would forever rather have their presence in my life— irritating crap included—than not have them around.

So, the next time you find yourself in a tiff with your daughter, son, spouse, or friend, wishing they'd do something "better," "different," or "your way," ask yourself: Would I rather have a clean room or an empty one?

Do the Work
Choosing Gratitude Over Frustration

What things do you often find yourself annoyed at others over?

How do you prevent minor issues from driving a wedge between you and your loved ones?

What family-related things often make you mad?

What could you do today to practice turning annoyance at others' actions into gratitude?

Journal Notes

_____

_____

_____

_____

_____

_____

_____

_____

_____

_____

_____

_____

_____

_____

_____

_____

_____

_____

_____

_____

_____

Chapter Eight
Everyone Does the Best They Can

My parents had four kids at twenty-one and nineteen years old, respectively.

And with four kids, they made the bold choice to move across the country with no family support because the town we lived in when I was born was very dangerous. They wanted better for us.

It was a challenging move for the whole family, and I'm sure my parents often wondered if they were making the right decision. Many fights, tensions, resentments, and challenging changes occurred during that period in our family's history.

Today, that city has one of the highest crime rates in America: 46 per 1,000 residents.

To put that in perspective, they moved us to Dixon, IL—with a crime rate of 2.5 per 1,000 residents.

So, my parents obviously made the right decision, despite how hard it was.

Because of that brave move to a strange new city, my siblings and I were afforded new opportunities in a safe place.

But this is the kind of thing I only appreciate now, as an adult with kids of my own.

Growing up, I resented my parents for all sorts of reasons. My mom and I had a rocky relationship for much of my childhood and young adult life.

Looking back on that time now, I'm filled with gratitude for both of my parents. I'm forever thankful for my father's work ethic and his strong sense of responsibility for his family. I'm grateful that he cared enough about us to work every day to ensure that we always had food on the table and a roof over our heads. And I'm grateful to our mom for keeping a clean house and providing clean clothes and home-cooked meals.

My parents did the very best they could with what they had.

I honestly can't even imagine how difficult life was for them was at that time. I wonder if I could have done the same without losing my mind or, at best, having a complete nervous breakdown.

Despite how hard it got for them, they always did their best. And I think they did a pretty bang-up job; all of my siblings and I have turned into pretty cool, successful, well-adjusted adults.

Perspective has changed my attitude from anger to gratitude and understanding. I no longer choose to focus on the parts of my childhood that brought me pain. Instead, I focus on all I had and everything I am grateful for. I'm thankful for the opportunities given to me.

I've learned that time and perspective give us a new sense of appreciation for the struggles in our lives, and they also give us gentle compassion for others. But whether you have the perspective to understand a person's actions, or you're confused and feeling resentful because of it, the best thing you can do is repeat this mantra: "They're doing the best they can."

And when you genuinely start to believe it and give people the benefit of the doubt, magic happens.

Do the Work
Practicing Grace

Take a minute to think about a situation in which you've resented someone (or maybe actively resent them still) for their actions.

Practice extending grace to them by saying aloud, "They did the best they could." Does it feel sincere to say this about them? Why or why not?

Think back to a situation where you feel you made a wrong decision or are ashamed of your actions. Practice extending grace to yourself by saying out loud, "I did the best I could." Does it feel sincere to say this about yourself? Why or why not?

Write down a list of your own perceived benefits of extending grace by assuming that people are doing their best. Remember to recall this list when you feel resentment, anger, or confusion about a person's actions.

Journal Notes

_____

_____

_____

_____

_____

_____

_____

_____

_____

_____

_____

_____

_____

_____

_____

_____

_____

_____

_____

Chapter Nine
Time is Your Most Valuable Resource

"You live as if you were destined to live forever, no thought of your frailty ever enters your head, of how much time has already gone by you take no heed. You squander time as if you drew from a full and abundant supply, though all the while that day which you bestow on some person or thing is perhaps your last."

Seneca

Today, the average person in the United States lives to be seventy-six years old. That equates to 27,740 days total. If you're in your thirties reading this, you've already lived over 10,000 of those days.

How does that make you feel?

As I've gotten older, my sensitivity to time has increased. I don't sit around thinking about how many days I have left, but I do think about how much time I've squandered, pretending that time is an infinite resource.

We don't know how much time is given to us. That's a tragedy of life.

A bittersweet truth to go along with that is that if today, you lost everything you own and everyone you love was taken from you, all you'd have left is time. Your precious time—to spend or waste as you wish. Who knows how much time you'll have… shouldn't you make the most of it?

I've found the best way to spend my time in my life is to figure out what I value most and dedicate ample time to those things. This might sound trivial, but it's much more poignant in application.

Take some time today to write out what you value most in your life. Next to each item, activity, or person, write the average percentage of time you think you spend enjoying them. Do you see an imbalance somewhere or an opportunity to spend more time on a certain one?

Your time is a gift. Spend it wisely. You can create whatever life you want. You have time (for now).

Decide what matters to you and dedicate your time to it. Relaxation? Peace? Productivity? Making memories with your family? Building a legacy? Eating delicious food and swimming in the ocean? Give your precious time to these things and enjoy each moment.

Do the Work
Balancing Your Time Books

What have you identified as the most valuable ways to spend your time? (e.g., time spent with family, time spent doing hobbies, time spent learning or teaching, etc.)

Do you feel like you're spending enough time (or perhaps too much) on any of these items? Does your "timesheet" feel unbalanced?

How can you work on spreading out your time more evenly among the things you like doing the most?

Before going to sleep tonight, ask yourself this question: "Am I proud of how I spent my time today?" Begin to make it a habit of asking yourself this each night before bed.

Journal Notes

_____

_____

_____

_____

_____

_____

_____

_____

_____

_____

_____

_____

_____

_____

_____

_____

_____

_____

_____

_____

_____

Chapter Ten
Date Yourself First

When my daughter was in fourth grade, she came home and told me her friend had a boyfriend.

I recognized this as a "teachable" moment.

I asked her to explain what she meant by "have a boyfriend."

She didn't have too much to say; it just meant they liked each other.

Having been a fourth-grader myself once, I knew that it was around this age that the pressure to "fit in" would start to kick in for my daughter and her peers. She likely wanted to talk about it because she thought she should be getting a boyfriend, too.

Now, of course, a fourth-grade dating relationship would never be very serious or hold much substance. But I wanted my daughter to understand what relationships are and what it means to be in one.

This was the perfect moment to teach her about "dating" herself. To really understand her emotions and how they change. To understand what made her feel sad, happy, lonely, or engaged. To start to foster a sense of authentic self-worth and intrinsic appreciation for herself so that one day in the future, she could be in a healthy, fulfilling dating relationship with someone else.

Most importantly, I wanted her to understand that she should enter a relationship because she wanted to, not because she felt pressured to.

I've seen too many women and young girls jump from relationship to relationship simply because they couldn't be alone.

Those kinds of relationships almost always fail; and if they don't, they're incredibly toxic. They can cause a lifetime of pain and regret.

But dating yourself—entering into a serious relationship with yourself—is arguably one of the most important things you can do for the quality of the other relationships in your life. You learn what you like and dislike, how to get your needs met, and how to fulfill your own happiness. When you really get the hang of this (which, by the way, takes a lifetime to perfect, so don't rush it and be hard on yourself while you're learning!), you can be a great partner and have a truly fulfilling relationship with another person.

I'm glad I taught my daughter this lesson in the fourth grade. She's getting pretty good at meeting her own needs, and that makes me a very happy mom!

Do the Work
Dating Yourself First

Think about the best friend you've ever had. What is it about that relationship that makes you feel so good? Do they possess qualities you'd like to foster in yourself?

What can you do today to practice dating yourself? Increase your self-care? Spend some time in meditation to listen to your needs? Take yourself out for a super-fun date? Try to be a great "date" for yourself today.

Imagine you are knocking on your own door with flowers in your hand, asking yourself on a date. Would you be impressed, intrigued, and excited to date you? Or would you be turned off by this "date"? Take some time to think about why this is.

Journal Notes

_____

_____

_____

_____

_____

_____

_____

_____

_____

_____

_____

_____

_____

_____

_____

_____

_____

_____

_____

Chapter Eleven
Who is the "You" that Everyone Else Sees?

You've probably said (or at least thought) multiple times in your life that you want to be "a more authentic self." But which "self" are you talking about when you say this?

Is it the version of you that shows up during those fleeting moments in life when the stars align and life feels like a dream come true? Is it the one that shows up after a stressful day and can't handle much more pressure? Is it the one that sometimes feels humbled by gratitude and grace and softly accepts life on life's terms? Or is it the one that shows up and speaks to us from the recesses of our hearts when we are ridden with grief, anxiety, or depression?

Which "you" is the real you?

The answer is *all of them*.

These different forms of you have all been formed by your life experiences. They've protected, emboldened, supported, and challenged you when you needed it. They've acted as defense mechanisms in scary times or been your salvation when you felt like you'd lost all hope. They've helped you express emotions and memories you kept trapped inside you when it was time to release them.

All of these pieces of you have been born out of a purpose: to help you live a safe and productive life. Even the ones you don't like.

So, how often do you think about which "you" the people in your life see?

If you care what people think of you (and most of us are guilty of this at some point), you've probably thought of it often.

Do the Work
Who is the "You" that Everyone Else Sees?

Write down everything you think people "see" when they see you. Do they see a healthy, confident person? Do they see someone who has it all together? Do they see someone who's transparent and open about their struggles? Or do they see a mess that they feel pity for? Write down all the things you think others observe about you.

Now, what do *you* see when you look in the mirror? Do you see yourself as strong, confident, and winning in life? Do you see someone struggling to get through the day? Maybe you see someone who's constantly dropping the ball and failing at life. Write down all the ways you feel like you've been showing up as "you" lately.

Are the "you" that you think others see and the "you" that you believe yourself to be the same person? Chances are, they're not. I've done this exercise with dozens of people and have yet to come across someone whose two sides look the same.

The critical takeaway from this lesson is that the authentic "you" that is made up of many facets can be the same "you" you show to others. It's a myth that we must show up as any particular, steady version of ourselves for others to accept us. You are the same "you" when you are in "survival mode" as the "you" that sometimes feels very confident—they're just different sides of the same coin. Everyone that you know has all these different sides, too.

When you can show up "authentically" with people, gently accepting and showing each side of yourself, you'll find that others will feel more comfortable doing the same.

Journal Notes

_____

_____

_____

_____

_____

_____

_____

_____

_____

_____

_____

_____

_____

_____

_____

_____

_____

_____

_____

_____

_____

Chapter Twelve
The People Who Keep Showing Up for You

"If you live to be a hundred, I want to
live to be a hundred minus one day, so
I never have to live without you."

Winnie the Pooh

I met my best friend Judy B. in middle school.

We were the most unlikely friends you could imagine. Judy is kind and soft-spoken. I am the opposite of soft-spoken but do consider myself pretty kind.

Judy spent her spare time in the bowling alley. I spent mine in the Smoker's Alley of our high school.

Judy always did the right thing and tried to keep her nose clean. I was always looking for trouble.

Despite our differences, we became inseparable very quickly for one simple reason: Judy always showed up.

When I needed her. When she needed me. When I was lonely. When she was lonely. Through good times and bad, Judy was always there.

She has been a constant in my life since middle school. She's the first person I call when I need advice or comfort, and she has always accepted me just as I am. What a gift!

There's a common saying about the phenomenon of people coming into our lives: that they show up for a reason, a season, or a lifetime.

At fifty, I know without a doubt that lifetime friends are scarce and extremely valuable.

If you have a blessed life, you've been blessed with someone who always shows up. They make an effort. They stay in touch. They hold space for you when you need to grow on your own and push you when you need to be pushed.

Don't take this person for granted. They're one of life's most precious gifts. And if you are one of these lifetime friends for someone else, know this: You are a tremendous blessing to your loved one. Feel great about that today!

Do the Work
Appreciating Your Lifetime Friends

Write a list of the people in your life who always show up.

Write a list of the people you always show up for.

Reflect on how you can better appreciate your friends who always show up.

What makes you want to show up for the people in your life?

Why do you think your friends always show up for you?

Do something today to show your lifetime friends that you appreciate them—send them a message or a gift, or make a plan to do something fun together.

Journal Notes

_____

_____

_____

_____

_____

_____

_____

_____

_____

_____

_____

_____

_____

_____

_____

_____

_____

_____

_____

_____

Chapter Thirteen
You're Not a Victim in Your Story

When my daughter was moving into her new apartment for school, she and her boyfriend who was helping both got parking tickets. And not just passive parking tickets—the officer had put tire locks on their vehicles along with the tickets on the windshields.

She, of course, felt compelled to pay for her boyfriend's ticket because he was only there to help her. Combined, the fees were $200. $200 is a lot of money for a college student.

She called me in hysterics, crying and hyperventilating.

I simply said to her, "Honey, it's going to be okay. Shit happens. When it comes to things like this in life, you have to understand that it's not a matter of whether you will ever get a parking or a speeding ticket. It's *when* you will get one. It's just one of those things in life that you need to know will likely happen. And you know what? It's okay. It's not the end of the world. Yes, it sucks, and it's expensive, and it is tough to hand over your hard-earned money. But in the grand scheme of things, this too shall pass. So, take a deep breath and let it go. Everything will be all right."

Of course, this lesson didn't feel so great to her at the time. After all, she still had to shell out $200. However, she remembered the lesson afterward and I believe it helped her manage her expectations of what life would bring her.

Whether it's a speeding ticket, parking ticket, a late fee, or a failed grade on a test, it's important not to let the occurrences of life spin you out of control.

You're not a victim in your life. Sometimes, things happen because you do something stupid; sometimes, things happen for no reason.

The thing that's always in your control is how you react to it. And staying cool and calm is always the easier way to navigate the storm.

Do the Work
Slaying Your Victim Mentality

When shit happens, what are the first emotions you feel? Write an uncensored list. Don't think too hard about this. Write everything that you experience when something terrible happens in your life.

Look at the list of things you feel when shit happens. Make a note of how many of these emotions feel "helpless" ("It's unfair that this is happening to me," "I don't know what to do," etc.) and how many of them feel like "acceptance" (resignation, determination to fix it, bravery, etc.). Don't judge yourself if you feel more "helpless" emotions. Just take note of it.

Looking at the emotions you feel when bad stuff happens, do you see one or two you can quickly work on overcoming or changing? Begin a practice of narrowing in and working on this particular emotion. Celebrate small steps of progress toward "acceptance." Great work, you!

Journal Notes

_____

_____

_____

_____

_____

_____

_____

_____

_____

_____

_____

_____

_____

_____

_____

_____

_____

_____

_____

Chapter Fourteen
How to Live the Life You Want

Grocery shopping, college applications, romantic partners: What do these things have in common?

Everyone in your life will have lots to say about how you should do all of these.

Don't get me wrong: Having a solid support system around you to positively influence and give you good advice is vital.

But when was the last time you chose something just because *you* wanted it?

Life is a series of choices and random outcomes. We all know this. Make a choice. See how it turns out.

Some of us turn to others for help in making our decisions because there's a lot to consider, or we struggle with knowing what the "right" choice is.

But at the end of the day, do you trust yourself to make the best choice for your life?

When you consider where you are in your life—your current job, the city you live in, how you're raising your kids, who you're married to, what you say and don't say in public—

do you feel like all of these things are authentically "you?" Chosen by you, boldly and bravely?

Or have you "gone along" with the choices someone else encouraged you to make?

If it's the former, congrats—you're living the life you made.

If it's the latter, relax—you're a totally normal human who respects the opinions of those around you.

But here's a challenge for you if you feel like a lot of the choices in your life have been made or heavily influenced by someone else: Today, you're going to make some choices just for you because *you* want it.

This might sound trivial, but hear me out. Like any other skill in life, this takes practice;and starting small is the ticket to enormous success.

Do the Work
Practicing Choosing for Yourself

Out of the following "categories" in your life, which do you feel has been most heavily influenced by other people?

- child-rearing
- your job
- your free time
- your daily routine
- your political views

Whichever category you choose, ask yourself the following questions:

- Who is the person that most heavily influences my decisions/beliefs in this category?

- Why do I trust their opinion?

- Do I feel we have an equal say in decisions in this area of my life?

- If not, how can I reclaim some of my power and start speaking up for myself?

Now that you've identified the What, the Who, and the Why, challenge yourself to make three decisions in this category of your life—on your own—this week. If you feel that this might cause a problem, explain to your partner/influence why this is important to you. Give specifics so that they understand you better.

After your three decisions have been made and followed through, reflect on how they went. How did your partner/influence react to you completing the decision independently? How did the decision play out for you? Do you regret your decision, or was it empowering? What would you do differently in the future?

Continue to practice making choices just for you, made by you. Start small and build this skill.

Journal Notes

_____

_____

_____

_____

_____

_____

_____

_____

_____

_____

_____

_____

_____

_____

_____

_____

_____

_____

Chapter Fifteen
Heartbreak Means It Mattered

Heartbreak happens. It's a matter not of *if* but *when*.

Heartbreak is part of being human. If you care about people and situations, you will be heartbroken by both of these at some point.

Sickness, death, betrayal, loss, rejection, failure—it comes in many forms.

How depressing, right?

Actually, it can be pretty lovely once it's reframed in your mind.

Since we know that heartbreak is inevitable, we must learn to live with it and process it in healthy ways.

Heartbreak comes from caring. You care because something or someone brought value to your life. This situation or person has taught you more about yourself—what's important to you and what makes you feel good, accomplished, fulfilled—and so you can use that info to search out more of the same in other areas of your life.

When you reframe heartbreak from a place of gratitude, it goes something like this: "I am hurting because this ___ meant a lot to me. I'm grateful that I had it. I treasure the [lessons, time, value, love, skills, happiness, etc.] it gave me. I understand that I can find this type of ___ again—and now I know better what I'm looking for."

Heartbreak is returning to the valley after a beautiful view from the mountaintop. You learn to appreciate the view from up high much more when you're on the ground again.

Do the Work
Reframing Heartbreak

Think back to a heartbreak that happened long enough ago that it doesn't sting anymore. What did you learn from it? What good has since come from that heartbreak?

Consider a situation you're currently in that could cause you heartbreak in the future. Take a moment to imagine and *experience* the heartbreak that could happen. Make a note of the emotions that come up. Write down the imagined heartbreak and the feelings you feel.

Now, try reframing this imagined heartbreak in a positive light. What good could come from this situation falling apart? What can be learned?

Journal Notes

_____

_____

_____

_____

_____

_____

_____

_____

_____

_____

_____

_____

_____

_____

_____

_____

_____

_____

_____

Chapter Sixteen
Resilience is a Muscle

We've all heard the saying, "Tough times build strong people."

Sure, but how do these strong people make it through the tough times? Do they curl up in a ball and wait for it to be over? Do they run in the opposite direction of the tough time until it catches up with them and then submit to it in shame?

No. Obviously not.

Strong people are strong because they've developed resilience. And resilience is built like a muscle— through practice.

If you're listening closely enough to someone talking about a tough time they went through, you'll hear them say a mantra or a thought they held onto to keep them moving through the challenge.

Mine was: "For now... not forever."

To me, this means that I accept that this shitty thing is happening, but it won't always be happening. It's another take on "this, too, shall pass." Time passes. This tough time will pass.

But telling myself, "For now... not forever" is just the kickoff point.

After all, the time will pass, but how I *use* the time is what really matters.

And here's where the resilience muscle begins to be built.

I came up against two monsters during any tough time I faced: the first was Fear and the second was Lack of Confidence.

Fear of the unknown. Fear of failure. Fear of being hurt, judged, taken advantage of. Fear of never recovering from this challenge. Fear of falling behind.

And my lack of confidence showed up and tested me in lots of ways, dancing with this fear in a dizzying tango that made me feel paralyzed.

These days, when I come up against challenging situations, I try to practice these three Resilience-Building Steps:

1. I say my mantra: "For now. Not forever." This is acceptance. Acceptance brings some peace to my soul. I'm not fighting. I'm not running away. I'm ready to take a closer look at the situation.

2. I acknowledge the things I'm afraid of about this situation. This prevents catastrophizing. It helps to literally write down every possible way this challenge could go wrong and then decide how many of them are rational. Then I can build a plan to tackle the fear and possible worst-case scenarios, which also helps assuage the fear.

3. I remember that confidence is built, just like resilience. And it's built by rising to challenges. Trying new things. Testing out theories. Being willing to be afraid and take action anyway. So, I take an unsteady, unsure step in the direction I think is best. And my confidence grows.

These steps have taken a long time to be developed, and they're certainly not perfectly habitual. I come up against new scary challenges every day. And sometimes, I'm overwhelmed by fear. Sometimes I have no confidence. Sometimes I forget to tell myself that this is a temporary situation.

But I find that when I can muster at least two of these three Resilience Building steps, I can rise to the challenge. Try it yourself this week!

Do the Work
Build Your Resilience Muscle
with These Steps

Develop a mantra you can say to yourself when things get tough—something you can say to yourself that motivates, empowers, and strengthens you. I don't care how cheesy you think this is; it will be important when you get knocked over by the waves of life.

Think about all the things that scare you about a current challenging situation. Imagine every way it could go wrong. Write it all down: the things that make you nervous, unsure, and unsteady. Get it all down on paper. Now, look at your list and ask yourself, "How many of these are really going to happen?"

Imagine your confidence and resilience as a baby muscle in this situation. What step can you take to make this muscle stronger? What past experience can you draw on to make you feel more prepared for this situation? Is there something you can do today to feel more confident in this situation? If so, do that thing today!

Journal Notes

_____

_____

_____

_____

_____

_____

_____

_____

_____

_____

_____

_____

_____

_____

_____

_____

_____

_____

_____

_____

_____

Chapter Seventeen
The First Step Always Sucks the Hardest

What is something you want to do but haven't done yet?

This isn't a "fluff" question. I want you to think about it for a minute.

When you were young, you had many dreams of what you wanted to be/thought you could be/dreamed of being/doing/having.

And then, you grew up and slowly started to let go of your dreams, one by one.

I mean, I'm sure you've achieved some of your dreams.

But we all have dreams from when we were little that we've since abandoned. Some of them were crazy, and we grew out of them. Others, we talked ourselves out of as we grew older, but those dreams spoke to our innermost desires to achieve great things.

Regardless of what your dreams are (or were), here's something to consider: The first step toward reaching a dream always sucks the hardest. The most challenging part of achieving your dream is making your first move toward it.

The first step will always be your longest stride.

Here's why: When you head in the direction of a dream, you've already conquered your mind, your fear, and any defeatist beliefs you might have about deserving or achieving it.

You've stopped listening to the voices of those around you who tell you to "be realistic" or "it's already been done" or "are you sure that's what you want?"

And conquering those things is the hardest part of heading toward a dream.

Full stop.

Whether it's losing twenty pounds, asking out someone you consider "out of your league," quitting your job to start a non-profit or becoming a roller derby superstar, the most challenging step you'll take is the first one.

Once you do that, you'll see where you should go next. You'll feel more confident in your ability to do scary stuff.

So, what have you been putting off taking the first step of?

Do the Work
Find Your First Step

What do you want to accomplish this year? Think of one big task, dream, life change, etc.

Now, plot out what the first step to do would be. It might not be "applying for the job." It might be something less obvious, like tackling your belief in whether or not you can actually do it or doing the research to find out what's actually involved. Chances are, your subconscious already knows what the first step should be and it's scary because it will require tackling something you are afraid of.

Make a commitment to yourself to take the first step. Put a timeframe on it to keep yourself accountable. If you can, keep a journal of the experience so that you begin to understand the patterns of fear and hesitation your mind throws at you before you accomplish a scary thing. This will be helpful to look back on in the future!

Journal Notes

_____

_____

_____

_____

_____

_____

_____

_____

_____

_____

_____

_____

_____

_____

_____

_____

_____

_____

_____

_____

Chapter Eighteen
Act Like You Live in the Future, Now

I have a friend who, for the past six months, has been living on a farm as a part-time farmhand while building her writing business. Her life is filled with exciting opportunities to learn and try new things, and she's found great fulfillment from living life on her own terms.

Six months ago, though, her life looked very, very different.

She lived in a tiny basement apartment and was in a long-term relationship she knew wasn't suitable for her.

She had a deep longing to connect with nature and try out something new in a new place, but she felt stuck in her life as it was.

She told me about how she wanted to make a change in her life, but she didn't know how to do it. She was afraid of breaking her boyfriend's heart; she was scared of starting over, of trying something new.

But she wanted it badly enough that she was ready to be brave and she asked for my advice on how to take the first step.

My advice to her was this: "Act as if you're already living in your future. Be the person you want to be in your new life."

Of course, I couldn't give her any specific advice about who that person was because only she knew that, but she understood what I was saying.

A few days later, she wrote to me to share that she'd started making minor changes to be her future self. She told her boyfriend that she wanted to focus on her own needs, listen to her favorite music more often, and spend more time doing her hobbies.

She said something miraculous started to happen: As she embraced living as her new future self, she got braver about making changes in her life.

She started to picture her new life and took steps in its direction.

She ended the relationship that she knew wasn't right for her.

She started looking at options for being more connected with nature. Soon, she was in touch with a family friend who owned a farm in another state; and as a beautiful coincidence, this family friend was looking for someone to come live on the farm and help with the upcoming harvest season.

Once she made the changes to step into who she wanted to be, the pieces started to fall into place. The image in her mind began to manifest in her real life.

The changes began with *her*—from her choice to start acting like she was already living in her future.

Who do you want to be in the future? Start acting like it today. Watch the magic happen.

Do the Work
Living as the Future You

Do you have a long-term goal for your life that will require a lot of personal changes? If yes, write down that goal.

Now, picture the Future You that has accomplished this goal. Is that person more focused, determined, resilient, and carefree? Write down the most robust and positive characteristics Future You is proud to possess.

What daily activities does Future You do to foster these strong positive characteristics? Write down the daily habits, mantras, or beliefs that Future You does to feel deeply grounded in self.

Finally, write down something you can start doing *today* to become Future You. Is it practicing forgiveness instead of holding onto grudges? Being braver about scary things? Speaking up and practicing sharing your opinion? Or maybe something more tangible, like getting into a hobby that you know Future You loves to do in your Future Life?

Make a promise to yourself to do one thing daily to help build Future You.

Journal Notes

_____

_____

_____

_____

_____

_____

_____

_____

_____

_____

_____

_____

_____

_____

_____

_____

_____

_____

_____

   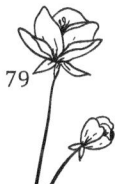  

Chapter Nineteen
You Only Fail
If You Quit

There is something we so often forget about everything that has ever been accomplished: At some point during the creation phase of that accomplishment (invention of the airplane, electricity, discovering the cure for polio, discovering new countries, etc.), the person or people involved wanted to give up and quit trying—many times over.

We can refer to thousands of success stories with the underlying theme that the option to give up was presented repeatedly—and it was a tempting one.

But the only reason we know about those successes is that each person just simply refused to quit.

You can guarantee that it was a really tough decision to keep going, but they did it.

Each person that accomplished something hard found their own reasons. Some of them, I'm sure, seemed absolutely absurd to any onlookers:

- They had already sunk so much time into the project that they couldn't stand the thought of not finishing;

- They had nothing else to do with their
  time, so they just kept going;

- They grew so angry at consistently coming up
  short or someone telling them they were going
  to fail that they were literally fueled by rage;

- They were the last ones still working on
  it,and their pride wouldn't let them stop.

Each person found their reason to keep going, and they didn't fail because they simply didn't quit.

Some of them probably felt like failures through the entire process. They had not a single drop of motivation or inspiration left. Still, they just made a habit of continuing until it was finished.

The thing we so often forget about everything that's ever been accomplished is this: You only fail if you quit.

If you're on the precipice of starting a new project, stopping a bad habit, making a significant life change, or discovering something new, do yourself a favor and accept this truth: You're going to struggle consistently when working to achieve a goal. Find your reason to keep going and just keep going, no matter how insane it sometimes feels.

Do the Work
Find Your Reason Not to Quit

In the previous "Do the Work" section, you identified a long-term goal you'd like to reach. Recall that goal for this exercise.

Write down all the reasons you want to achieve that goal on a piece of paper. They can be as silly or serious as you want them to be! Just write down every single reason for reaching your goal until you can't think of any more.

From this list, choose one that feels the most like it will keep you going. If you can't choose just one, pick three in total.

Write down your reason or reasons for not quitting on a separate piece of paper—somewhere you can easily see them or refer to them when you want to give up.

Make a promise to yourself that for the reason(s) you've listed, no matter how discouraged you feel or how many snags you hit, you will continue to obsessively reach for your goal.

Journal Notes

_____

_____

_____

_____

_____

_____

_____

_____

_____

_____

_____

_____

_____

_____

_____

_____

_____

_____

_____

_____

_____

_____

_____

Chapter Twenty
Rumination is a Choice

Have you ever heard stories of people who overcame utter heartbreak, terrifying illness, or desperately hard times, and then went on to do amazing things for other people despite their struggles?

These stories are inspiring, to be sure. But often, we think to ourselves (quietly), "I don't know if I would be able to do that if I were in their shoes."

We often fail to consider, at first pass, that people who overcome great suffering to do something incredible aren't stronger than us or more capable or bullheaded.

They simply chose not to ruminate.

What is rumination, exactly?

Rumination occurs when something terrible happens and we spend a great deal of time going over and over it in our minds. Passing through each detail, we suffer the event repeatedly, even long after it's happened.

I'm sure you've done your fair share of ruminating over lousy stuff. I know I have.

Why do we ruminate on stuff, anyways? Here's what the research says.

According to a research piece published in 2016, rumination is categorized as an "attentional deployment technique… considered a type of cognitive avoidance strategy" (Ragen, Roach, Chollak; Chronic Stress, Regulation of Emotion, and Functional Activity of the Brain; Academic Press, 2016).

Did you catch that?

It's considered *avoidance strategy* because when you're ruminating, you're not accepting the circumstances of your life. And as they say: Acceptance is the first step.

Sometimes, it feels like rumination is an obsessive study of the patterns of an event to prevent it from happening in the future and therefore has to have some value.

In fact, rumination often feels good. Why? Because instead of suffering the effect of the event over and over again. We look at all the details surrounding it as if we could change any of them to make it so the event never happened. But just like picking at a scab, this doesn't actually achieve anything. In fact, it slows down the healing process.

People who achieve great things don't allow themselves time to ruminate on failure. Sure, they feel the acutely painful effects; there's no avoiding that. But they don't continue to let themselves suffer the pain. They keep moving *despite* the pain (as mentioned in the previous chapter, "You Only Fail If You Quit").

Do the Work
Stopping Rumination in Its Tracks

Identify a traumatic event in your life (from the past!) that you spent a great deal of time replaying or reliving. Spend time focusing on the specific emotions you experienced while ruminating over the event. Write down these emotions.

Now, pause to consider what ruminating on that event actually did for you. On the same sheet of paper, write down a Pros and Cons list about how ruminating about the event benefited or harmed you. For instance, you may have learned a valuable life lesson by going over your own mistakes; or maybe you wasted time pitying yourself, becoming increasingly depressed and unmotivated, when you could have moved on to better ways of dealing with the event.

After looking at this list, consider whether you could have achieved the list items on the "Pro" side without ruminating. For instance, how can you identify a lesson to be learned or a character trait you can strengthen (or mitigate) without wasting time ruminating in the future? Write down your observations.

Journal Notes

_____

_____

_____

_____

_____

_____

_____

_____

_____

_____

_____

_____

_____

_____

_____

_____

_____

_____

_____

_____

   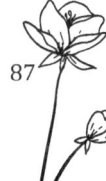  

Chapter Twenty-One
Stop Playing Life on Hard Mode

When you woke up this morning, you were tasked with something heavy and beautiful: what to do with the twenty-four hours ahead of you.

Life has asked you to show up. That's just how it is.

You were given the gift of breath and this nagging, demanding thing inside your mind—your consciousness—that expects you to make sense of everything around you and makes things impossibly difficult for you sometimes *because* it's trying to make sense of everything around you.

Simply being a human and being asked to do stuff and be stuff and think stuff and then, on top of all that, head in a direction and learn and make progress on stuff... it's a lot. And all of us—all of us—feel overwhelmed by it sometimes.

Now, as if it's not hard enough just being a human, everyone takes on responsibilities: raising children, being a loving family member, being a kind and honest citizen, being a helpful co-worker and employee, buying healthy food vs. eating takeout for the fifth time this week. We have constant decisions to make, and we have to deal with the outcomes.

We're playing life on the hard mode just by being alive, conscious, and trying to show up the best we can to shoulder the weight of the responsibilities we've chosen because no matter what we do or don't, life is going to throw us a metric shit-ton of hard times to handle.

Death, job loss, abandonment, rejection, breakups, your favorite Thai food place closing down; we can't foresee most of these sad, awful things, yet we're suddenly asked to deal with them, too.

Feels a bit bleak sometimes, doesn't it?

Here's the good news and a way to make your journey as a human much easier: We don't have to deal with the events of life gracefully. We can be a mess about our suffering, and it's totally justified (for a while). At some point, we are expected to pick ourselves back up and keep going. But despite what you might have been taught by parents, role models, or society, you are allowed to suffer through your suffering. Feel your pain. Mourn your losses. Let it be messy if it needs to be. It won't be forever. You will survive it as long as you don't quit.

The other side of the coin is that sometimes we hold on to our pain and suffering too tightly. We don't let it go when it's ready to leave. We let our pain define us, change us, make us bitter or resentful or afraid to take chances. This is doing Suffering on Hard Mode.

Here are some of the ways we hold on to suffering:

- Taking the words and actions of others personally (when most of the time, it has nothing to do with us)

- Making assumptions about the reason for our suffering ("I guess I deserved that," "Maybe this is karma," etc.)

- Jumping to the worst-case scenario of an event and experiencing fear, anxiety, or distress instead of being present for what's actually taking place

- Not managing our expectations of other people, situations, or outcomes, and then suffering disappointment when reality doesn't align with what we expected

- Comparing our journey to someone else's and feeling as if we "come up short."

- Holding on tightly to the end of something (breakup/job loss/friends moving away/death etc.) and refusing to accept that it has happened

My personal "tell" that I'm holding on tightly to suffering and making life harder than it needs to be is that when the acute emotions of an event or situation have passed, my mind is still searching for "meaning" or "something I missed" that I can feel miserable about (see the previous chapter, "Rumination is a Choice.")

You will have plenty of heartbreak and pain in your life. And each time, you will reach a point where you have the choice to level up, accept, and let go, or continue on suffering and play life in Hard Mode. Ask yourself this: "How can I make life easier on myself today?"

Do the Work
Letting It Be Easier

Consider the list of ways that we hold on tightly to suffering:

- Taking the words/actions of others personally

- Assigning "punishment" or making assumptions about the reason for our suffering (i.e., karma, etc.)

- Living in the worst-case scenario, even if it hasn't happened

- Unmanaged expectations

- Refusing to accept suffering

Think about a recent or current episode of suffering you have experienced/are experiencing. Have you been assigning any of the previous list items to this event? Consider them all and think carefully.

Once you've identified a way in which you're increasing your own suffering, make a plan to reduce or eliminate this "extra-hard homework" you've assigned to your suffering. For example, if you've realized you've been taking someone else's actions personally, choose to give them the benefit of the doubt by assuming their actions had nothing to do with you and release yourself from the pressure to suffer from their actions. Or maybe you've realized you've been "punishing" yourself for assuming that you "deserve" this most recent bout of suffering. Look closer at this belief. Why do you think you deserve it? Are you taking responsibility for the suffering that's not your fault? Can you distinguish between "the consequences of your actions" and a deep-seated belief that you "deserve" to feel pain or suffering? Write down whatever thoughts and observations you have.

Journal Notes

_____

_____

_____

_____

_____

_____

_____

_____

_____

_____

_____

_____

_____

_____

_____

_____

_____

_____

_____

_____

_____

Chapter Twenty-Two
Keep Asking "Why" and Live a Wild Life

Throughout this book, you've worked hard to shift your mindset on many things: setbacks, failures, losses, friendships, the opinions and actions of others, and your own potential.

The most significant gift in shifting your mindset is that you get the chance to be curious about another way of doing things and possibly discover a whole new set of paths laid out before you.

Human life is such an interesting phenomenon. It feels both an eternity long and impossibly short at the same time. If we're lucky, we get ninety years on Earth. From the time we come out of the womb, we look to the universe and others to confirm that we matter—that our presence here means something. We tell ourselves stories about why things happen like they do because our brains need to be constantly ordering and making sense of the events of our lives. We spend every waking minute trying to understand ourselves and others. We try to create meaning in our daily lives and hopefully learn how to love what we see.

Deep in our hearts, we know that time is our most precious resource, yet we waste so much of it doing useless, hurtful, meaningless things. But maybe part of the beauty of being human is that we have the freedom to waste time and we get to feel the consequences of wasting it. It's all part of the experiment. Choosing. Seeing what happens. Adjusting course when needed.

If you take nothing else from this book, let it be this: Keep questioning your reality. Keep asking "why" you do things a certain way. Keep wondering if the "way things have always been done" is the right way. Remain open to the possibility of doing everything differently. Take inspiration, lessons, and wisdom from everywhere and everyone you can. Never assume you understand. It's much more exciting if you don't, actually.

Bravery will come and go. Sometimes, you'll feel like you're on top of the world and you're ready to do the scariest thing you can think of; and other times, it will feel challenging to look closely at the thoughts inside your own mind. When you *can* be brave, always try to be—even if it's just to look closer at your own experience and emotions and pose a few questions about what you see.

When you're open and receptive to the many, varied, wild possibilities of life with all of its winding roads and valleys, you shatter the glass ceiling of reality. You can do whatever you want. You just have to think you can, and then you can.

May this shift in your mindset smash your own glass ceiling. Enjoy the journey, my friend.

Final Journal Notes and Thoughts

_____

_____

_____

_____

_____

_____

_____

_____

_____

_____

_____

_____

_____

_____

_____

_____

_____

_____

_____

Resources Page

Cover Photo by Jannes Jacobs @jannesjacobs

(Ragen, Roach, Chollak; Chronic Stress, Regulation of Emotion, and Functional Activity of the Brain; Academic Press, 2016).

About the Author

Belinda Egan is a Leadership Development Coach, Consultant, Speaker, and Digital Course Creator. Passionate about Leadership and Courageous Leadership's impact on the world, she wholeheartedly believes that until leaders can truly understand who they are at their core, they cannot affect lasting change in others. She believes the world needs more leaders ready to make a difference in the world. Life is a journey full of lessons, and it's in these lessons that we learn to lead with courage.

She lives in Arizona with her family, cavapoo Otis, miniature labradoodle Allie, and her tabby cat Angel. When she's not writing, building her online digital course, or working with clients, she enjoys having a glass of wine with a good book and making memories with her family and close friends.

You can learn more about Belinda on her website at https://belinda-egan.com

Acknowledgments

The inspiration to write this book came as I was approaching my 50th birthday. I'm passionate about the work I do in Leadership Development because I want to make a difference in the lives of people who are led by these leaders.

The desire to leave this world a better place than when I entered it runs deep. As I approached this milestone birthday, I also wanted the past five decades to mean something—to leave a legacy of lessons learned in hopes that others might find encouragement and hope for their journey.

Once I started writing, Alison Mitchell assisted me by helping me organize my thoughts and goals and making suggestions through her editing skills. Her dedication and commitment to helping me bring this book to life are appreciated and have allowed me to leave my mark on this world. And for that, I will be forever grateful.

https://alimitchellcopywriting.com/
ali-mitchell-copywriting

To my friends Tammy Helfrich, Kitty, Stolle, and Hailey Krajewski, who took the time to read my manuscript and give their honest and heartfelt testimonials. Thank you for being the type of friends who show up.

.

www.ingramcontent.com/pod-product-compliance
Lightning Source LLC
Chambersburg PA
CBHW060341130626
46553CB00003B/1071